Nuts, Nerds, & Savants

Neurodiversity & Creativity

Jimmy Huston

Cosworth Publishing

ISBN: 978-1-965153-39-0

Cosworth Publishing
21545 Yucatan Avenue
Woodland Hills CA 91364
www.cosworthpublishing.com

For information regarding permission,
please send an email to *office@cosworthpublishing.com.*

Dedicated to the Struggle

BAM!

Existence.

We're pretty sure it's here. We think it's real. Most of us. We can feel something solid under our feet. There is light, sound, a lot of water—that sort of stuff.

Sure, it was dark at first. That's why it's called the dawn of time. But that changed once things started popping. Cosmic dust. Massive bodies. Lots of collisions. Explosions. Fission. Fusion. Kaboom!

It's already infinite *and* it's expanding. Figure that out. It's cold. Absolute cold. Except when it heats up. Then it gets really, really hot.

Sparks fly. Well, *everything* flies in space. Then, before you know it (because you don't exist yet), it settles into a routine. Matter coalesces. Things collide. Other things clog together. Smaller things form big things. Big things get bigger. Get big enough, we call 'em a planet.

And then there's life.

Clearly there is life, or you wouldn't be reading this. We know what it takes. There are the building blocks. Just water (or ammonia) and a bunch of minerals, etc.

But it takes time. A lot of time. Then—eventually—you'll probably get something. Maybe one prokaryotic cell or so.

Conditions have to be right, of course. Perfect, actually. But, given an entire universe as a place and infinity as a time-frame, things will happen—like photosynthesis.

We get it. We don't quite understand it, but we get it.

Intelligence?

That's something else entirely. At a primal level, *something* is telling one cell to divide into two cells, even though that's not really intelligence. But things evolve. Then they crawl out of the ooze and start walking around looking for something to eat. That is problem solving, but not quite what we call thinking.

Yeah, there were a bunch of plants and animals, but let's skip ahead to what we consider to be people. Problem solving. Hunting. Agriculture. Architecture. Language. Travel. Lots of wars. That all comes from the brain. We know that, even though we hardly understand it. There are things going on in there. Neurons, nutrients, electricity, synapses. They do a pretty good job for the most part.

Eventually things got weird. People started coming up with stuff for no clear and practical reason. They liked certain noises, usually with a beat and repetitive melodies. Or, swatches of color that changed ordinary surfaces into images. Some were better at it than others, bringing us art, music, architecture, religion, and poetry.

That's just what brains do. Problem solving is fine as far as it goes, but eventually we start looking for enlightenment, or at the very least, entertainment.

All in all, things started looking pretty good. A good, healthy human brain can do a lot of things, but there are limits.

Going back to page one—"Bam! Existence" for instance—we don't really have a clue. We've mostly just settled on the compromise idea of a Big Bang, with the exception of a few myths about cosmic eggs, sun gods, watery chaos—and Genesis.

We still don't know zip.

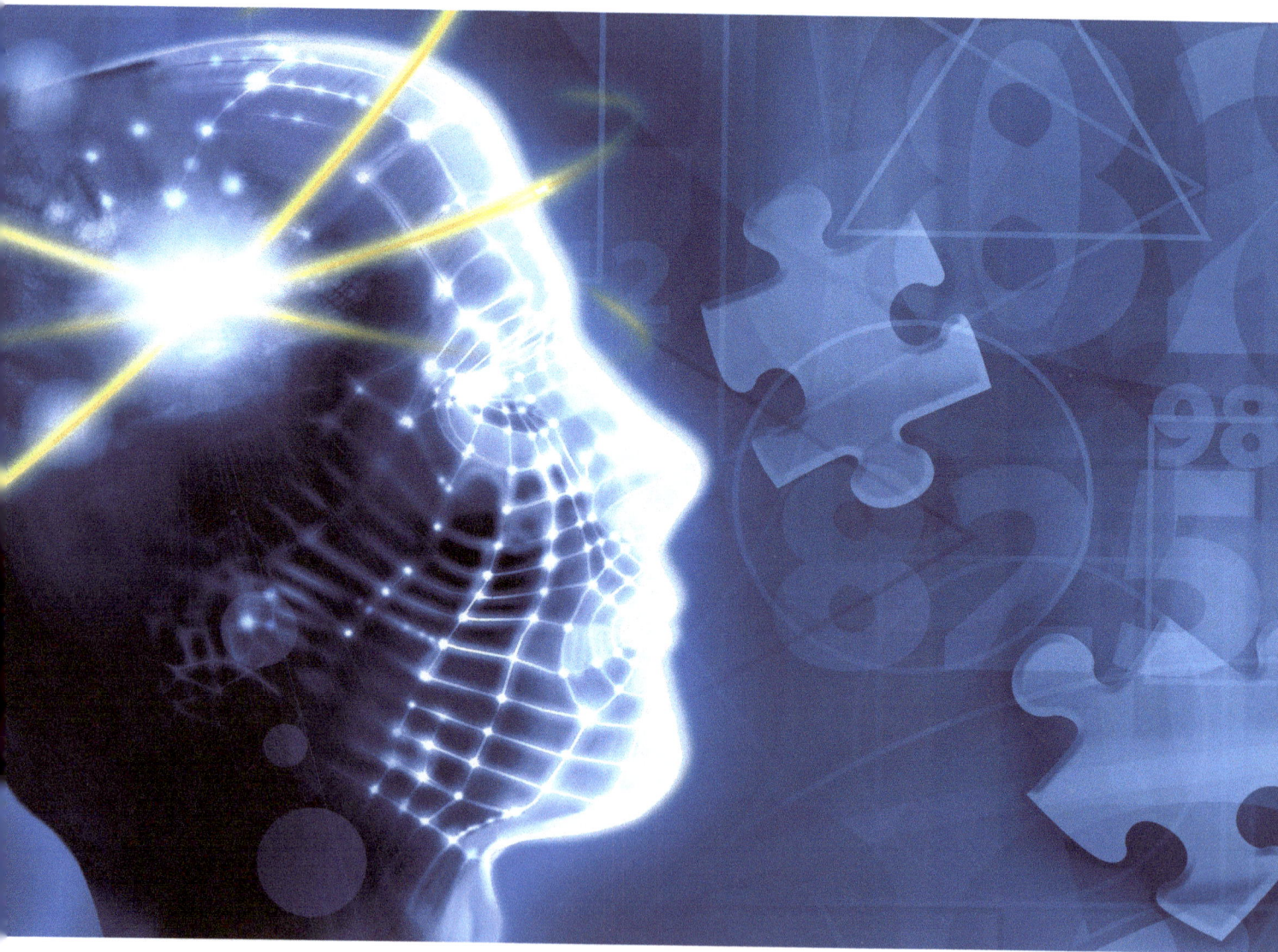

Moving on, we'll ignore the baffling, nonsensical concept of pre-existence and work on what we laughingly refer to as reality. That's something we can think about and, little by little, are starting to understand. We've gotten pretty good at a lot of things—feeding ourselves, transportation, medicine, engineering, even some limited space travel.

Along the way, there have been some roadblocks. Limits. Perhaps the first one was darkness. The first solution was to wait until morning. The next step was fire for torchlight, candles, and lanterns. Then eventually electricity. Admittedly there was quite a wait for electricity, but the more things improve, the harder the next stage is.

Electricity? Huh? What does *this* thing do?

Yikes!

When you're dealing with something as strange as electricity, it takes a certain type of mind to figure it out. (More on that later.)

Back to some other fields of interests. Early on, there wasn't much to do after dark, so multitudes of shepherds observed zillions of stars for millennia, but it takes a certain kind of mind to organize them into patterns. Why are they moving?

Chatting around the campfire led to philosophy and—somehow—mathematics. So the shepherds were the first astronomers, and somehow physics got involved, and then came astrology and the psychics. Just kidding. Skip them.

Navigation helped a lot, too. Discovering new lands didn't mean much if you couldn't find your way home. Things were different, depending on where you stood on the planet. Things in Africa weren't like they were in the Arctic. As people wandered, they exchanged seeds and spices and other stuff—and ideas.

There were some territorial disagreements along the way. Warfare is generally quite inventive. Some were better at it than others. Some were quite good at it, and they grabbed everything they wanted from everywhere they went, and took it home with them. They called that "trade."

People started making things. Simple and useful things at first. Pots. Candles. Axes. But, in time, there were machines. Actual mechanical devices that could do work.

Eventually there were automobiles. And flight. They figured out a way to walk through the sky. And they made automatic dishwashers, too. And electric tooth-brushes.

Jump ahead. Again, the next stage is always much harder. The limits are tougher. The speed of sound. Splitting the atom. Earth orbit. The moon. That may seem like the limit for now, but there are some pretty bright thinkers out there looking at Mars.

So here we are.

We're modern. We're even sort of futuristic. We're pretty smart, in general, but where did these ideas come from? Why did they take so long? When are the next ones coming along?

And, why do only some of us come up with the big ideas?

So that makes us wonder about creativity.

Uhm.... Creativity?

What is Creativity?

Well, there is normal A,B,C… etc., creativity. Or maybe A+B+C=D creativity, but that will *never* get you to $e=mc^2$.

What will? It's not just thinking out of the box—linearly. It's thinking some other way—spatially, laterally, diffusedly, hallucinogenicly, or even ecstatically, sometimes all at once. And that brings us to what is now called "neurodiversity."

Very early on, people noticed that someone was painting on the walls of their caves. And somebody came up with the first spear. Then there was the first person to make fire out of things that were not already hot. As Temple Grandin says, these were not the guys and gals outside the cave, chatting by the campfire.

They were probably ridiculed as the Cave Nerds.

We've all seen them. The brainiacs. The geniuses. The nerds.

They're rarely the suave playboy inventor like Robert Downey Jr. as Tony Stark in *Ironman*. True, they may stand out in the crowd, too, but it might be because they're twitching, or blinking, or rocking back and forth, or repeating themselves, or ignoring everyone around them, or dozens of other clues.

Why are *they* so smart?

But let's back up. A better question might be, "Why are they different?"

Simply put, they think differently because their brains are different—and now we call that being "neurodivergent."

General George Patton (ASD) famously stated, "If everybody is thinking alike, then somebody isn't thinking."

He's right. When everybody's mind is working in one direction, a neurodivergent thinker may be going in an entirely different direction—or dimension.

Were those ordinary shepherds creating physics and mathematics? Or were they super-shepherds?

For that matter, who were the architects of the pyramids, temples, and idols? Who created the tools and equipment that made them possible?

Hint: it wasn't the neurotypicals.

Just a minute. What is Neurodiversity?

In any shoe store you see a wide variety of footwear. There are work shoes, play shoes, and dress shoes for men, women, and children. That includes loafers, high heels, flip flops, saddle oxfords, moccasins, and shoes for tap dancing. There are shoes for running, jogging, walking, tennis, racquetball, basketball, and even driving. Cleated shoes for baseball, golf, and football have variations for wet or dry weather. Western cowboy boots differ from English-styled riding boots. Ballet slippers are not at all like combat boots. All shoes may be similar, but they have different characteristics.

Brains are like that, too, and come in an even wider variety. Some brains are good at math. Some are good with tools. Others easily become fluent in languages. Many have an interest in music. Some brains like to talk. Some definitely don't. Some change their interests constantly. Some are only interested in one area. Your peers, classmates, coworkers, and family are all different.

You've probably noticed that some people's brains are *really* different. That's what neurodivergent means. Those brains may be exceptionally good in math. Or, even better than that. Some brains are gifted in art. Some excel in the sciences, or invent things from fresh ideas. A lot of them excel in the world of music. And so forth.

Just like the rest of us, they're not good at everything. They are special, but not perfect. We all have idiosyncrasies which may be unusual or pronounced. So what? Their thinking is strong. Their ideas are often revolutionary. They are simply different.

Neurodiversity is not one thing. It's a continuum of behaviors that contains an entire spectrum—the Autism Spectrum Disorder—among things such as Dyslexia, Attention Deficit Hyperactivity Disorder, Obsessive Compulsive Disorder, Dyscalculia, Tourette Syndrome, Developmental Coordination Disorder, Dysgraphia, Intellectual Disability, Developmental Speech Disorder, Nonverbal Learning Disability, Epilepsy, and Bipolar Disorder.

These terms all have multiple behaviors and signs that can indicate a diagnosis. Some symptoms occur in more than one category, giving the appearance that one blends into the next. There also may be definite behaviors that do not occur in sufficient numbers or intensity to validate an official diagnosis. In other words, a person can fail to meet a formal diagnosis, yet still exhibit multiple symptoms sufficient to be considered OCD, ADHD, DCD, etc. by themselves or by others.

There have been some pretty smart people around for a very long time. We're still talking about some of them thousands of years later. In fact, we know so much about them from their peers that we believe they were neurodivergent long before it became fashionable. They were the early scientists, mathematicians, and philosophers. Pythagoras (ASD), Socrates (ADHD), Archimedes (ASD), and Hypatia of Alexandria (ASD).

Pythagoras

Socrates

Archimedes

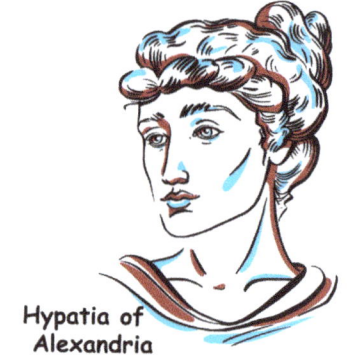
Hypatia of Alexandria

They were the pioneers of deep thinking. Their dialogues started conversations that are still going on today by our own geniuses. Over the centuries, there have been others, in many different fields.

People noticed that they were really bright, but they were often a little unusual. Sometimes it was minor, but sometimes it was extreme. Maybe they were preoccupied with their thoughts and ignored everyone. Maybe they were impatient with others, or even rude.

If they acted that way today, they might be classified as neurodivergent. So, let's do it. Let's make neurodivergence retroactive. It's not harmful, and the patterns that emerge could help us better understand some of the people around us today.

Many in this book are described with various types of neurodivergence, sometimes based on known facts, and sometimes based on popular discussions by non-experts. Any such label does not necessarily mean that someone *is* neurodivergent, but that some people think they are.

Neurodivergence is not an insult. It's a description, typically of observed behavior or actions. Even doctors and specialists can disagree on any diagnosis, but again, it's only an opinion, and anyone can have an opinion.

If you disagree, close the book. No harm done.

Still here? Okay.

Like it or not, now—as then—many of our best brains operate differently. It takes a certain kind of mind to actually think outside the box.

A Neurodivergent mind perhaps. While the human brain has to fit inside a pretty small skull, its thoughts can expand beyond all limits. Is it surprising that some expand beyond others?

Unconventional thoughts can yield visions, dreams, trances, illuminations, inspirations, perceptions, insights, premonitions, and transcendent breakthroughs. Somebody has to do it. Welcome the Neurodivergents. They bring eurekas galore.

Over the centuries our great thinkers have figured out that there are big, big heavenly bodies a long, long way away made of tiny, tiny particles that are made of much, much smaller bits. Galaxies and electrons. Planets and stardust. Hmmmm...

Yes, they've seen the similarities between neurons and lightning strikes. Big brains.

It all makes sense in a strange way if you don't think about it too hard. Some people are just better at this than others.

Yes, there are people who can conceive of things that are literally too large to be conceivable. Robert Oppenheimer (ASD). Stephen Hawking (ADHD). Galileo (ADHD). Benjamin Banneker (ASD). Albert Einstein (ASD). Issac Newton (ASD). Alan Turing (ASD). Michael Faraday (ASD). Carl Sagan (ASD). Neil deGrasse Tyson (ASD). Paul Dirac (ASD). Nerds? Certainly.

Does philosophy drive people crazy, or do those folks start a little out of the ordinary (untypical)? Think. About Bertrand Russell (ASD). Arthur Schopenhauer (ASD). Friedrich Nietzsche (ASD). Ludwig Wittgenstein (ASD). Immanuel Kant (ASD). Jean Paul Sartre (ASD). Baruch Spinoza (ASD). Nuts? Perhaps...

Neurodiversity. Sounds great. So what's the downside?

Before they're recognized for genius, they're known for their foibles. Apparently genius can lead to cranial overflow, spewing everything from minor eccentricities and quirks to major dysfunction.

That doesn't mean crazy, but hyperfocus on a previously unfathomable concept may result in unorthodox behavior. When you're wandering far out in the galaxy, lost among the stars, it doesn't matter if your socks don't match. If you're composing a symphony in your head, you may be late for dinner again—if you eat at all. When your quantum research is being ignored, maybe a tantrum is understandable. These brains are busy elsewhere.

And it's not just the geniuses at the top of the heap. There are the little guys whose thoughts struggle with OCD, ADHD, dyslexia, autism and more. Teachers. Mechanics. Soldiers. Bartenders. Farmers. They have good ideas, too. Maybe smaller good ideas, but needed ones. Solutions to real world problems. They keep us moving forward (even if they're a little nutty, too).

Creativity is not just dreaming big thoughts by the savants. Neurodiversity is inclusive. They are all around us, with unexpected good ideas, big and small.

SCIENTISTS start things off with insights and study. Then they try things. Again and again. And again and again. And again and again. Didn't work? Try it again. And again. Obsessive? Compulsive? Perhaps, but that's no disorder.

Louis Pasteur (ADHD). Paul Dirac (ASD). James Clerk Maxwell (ADHD). Carl Jung (ASD). Marie Curie (ASD). Alfred Kinsey (ASD). Dmitri Mendeleev (ASD). Michael Faraday (ASD). Barbara McClintock (ASD). Ivan Pavlov (ASD). Henry Cavendish (ASD). William Scott (ASD). Charles Darwin (ASD).

INVENTORS move things along, combining ideas in new ways. Alexander Graham Bell (ADHD). Thomas Edison (ADHD). Benjamin Franklin (ADHD). Wilbur Wright (ADHD). Woody Norris (ADHD). Alfred Nobel (Epilepsy). Nikola Tesla (ASD).

ENTREPRENEURS find a new way make it all work for everyone. Insight. Innovation. Henry Ford (ASD). Walt Disney (ADHD). Richard Branson (ADHD*). Howard Hughes (OCD). They helped to shape the future that we live in today. So what's next?

Are we moving into a future run by Neurodivergents? With their brain implants, Artificial Intelligence, and spaceships to Mars? Or are we already there?

Meet Mark Zuckerberg (ASD). Elon Musk (ASD*). Steve Jobs (ADHD). Bill Gates (ASD*). Jeff Bezos (ADHD). And get out of the way.

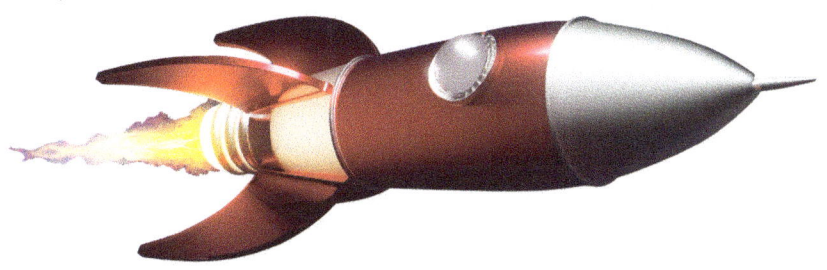

They left behind the old timey future of Jules Verne (ADHD). Aldous Huxley (ASD). George Orwell (ASD). H.G. Wells (ASD). H.P. Lovecraft (ASD). Anthony Burgess (ASD). Moving on....

* Denotes self-identified.

Many people may see a need, but when things are tough, only a few will find the way. Typically, they take pieces from many around them and put them together in a new way, finding a solution that works in the marketplace.

One of the necessary traits for these successful entrepreneurs is leadership—not something you think of for people on the spectrum or neurodivergent. A few quirks are not going to stop their quests.

Scientists comparing the hive-mind of ant colonies to the actions of groups of people noted that ant problem-solving improves with a large number of workers. And they found that's not true of people. (We all learn that on group projects in school.) People typically need a leader. If not a boss, at least someone who has a better idea than the groupthink.

LEADERS have to think differently. That certainly applies to governing. Winston Churchill (ADHD). Queen Elizabeth I (ADHD). Queen Elizabeth II (OCD). King Charles (ADHD). Vladimir Putin (ASD). Caesar Augustus (ASD). Robert F. Kennedy Sr. (ADHD). Nelson Rockefeller (Dyslexia). Al Gore (ASD). Jefferson Davis (ASD).

Maybe you've heard of these next few guys. They used to work in the government.

PRESIDENTS have no time for an average mind. They have to excel. George Washington (Dyslexia). Thomas Jefferson (ASD). Andrew Jackson (Dyslexia). Abraham Lincoln (ADHD). Ulysses S. Grant (ASD). Woodrow Wilson (Dyslexia). Dwight D. Eisenhower (Dyslexia). John F. Kennedy (Dyslexia). Lyndon B. Johnson (Dyslexia). Donald J. Trump (OCD).

WARRIORS do the fighting, but innovative thinking rules. General Eisenhower (Dyslexia). Emperor Napoleon (ASD). Julius Caesar (Epilepsy). General Custer (OCD). Alexander the Great (ADHD). General Montgomery (ASD). General Stonewall Jackson (ASD). General Grant (ASD). General Hannibal (ADHD). Saint Joan of Arc (Epilepsy). General Washington (Dyslexia). Nuts? Hardly.

Creative thinking pushes the limits of war—from crossbows to gunpowder to code breaking to remote viewing. Innovation ranges from the mind of Leonardo daVinci (ASD) to Edward Teller (ASD) and Robert Oppenheimer (ASD).

War isn't the way we want to go forward, but if it starts, we definitely want neurodivergent thinking on our side.

Are we smarter now than we used to be? We know more about some things, but that's because we have better tools today. We have the electron microscope. Magnetic Resonance Imaging. The Hubble telescope. Space stations.

The Sumerians didn't. Nor the Babylonians. Yet they figured out solstices and equinoxes. They named constellations.

We don't know how to build a pyramid like the ancients did. We've forgotten how to walk on water. We can't even read words carved in ancient stones.

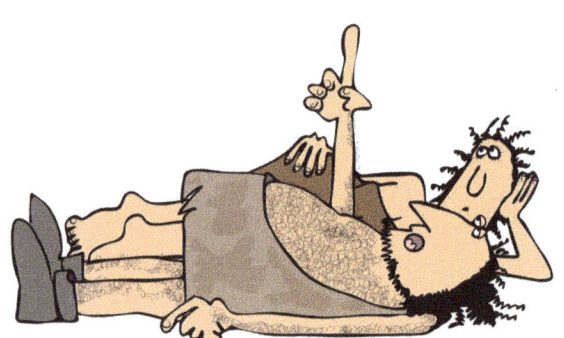

Were the ancients neurodivergent?

By and by, people like Galileo would start to figure things out, but he had to invent the telescope first.

Over the centuries, millions of people watched lightning in the sky. Only one guy decided to fly a kite in it. Hmmmm...

Time after time, it's one person who steps up with a new thought. Why?

It's simple. Neurodiversity is just another term for creativity.

Creativity is thinking differently. That's what the neurodiverse brain does. It works differently. In some ways better. In others, maybe not.

Thoughts may go in unusual directions. There may be distractions or diversions. There may be hyperfocus on some things and no focus on others. Neurons may wander. Synapses may surprise you. Daydreams may be solutions. Or hints.

Yet, there may be new thoughts. Innovation. Invention. Inspirations. Creatively speaking, neurodivergence can be a catalyst, an outlet. Answers.

The message is clear. Don't be afraid. Think up!

But it's not just science or warfare or religion that are evolving...

ART is quintessential creativity. Painters, sculptors, and others show us their unusual thoughts. Crucifixions. Madonnas. Sunflowers. Water lilies. Brillo pads. How do the masters look at things? What did they see differently? Why is perspective forced? Is color psychology? Is pointillism connected to atomic theory? Which pigments will endure for centuries? Is a toilet art? Is cubism neurodivergent?

Does being smart make a better artist? Leonardo da Vinci (ASD). Pablo Picasso (ASD). Michelangelo (ASD). Vincent van Gogh (ASD). Salvadore Dali (ASD). Rembrandt van Rijn (Bipolar). Stephen Wiltshire (ASD). Andy Warhol (ASD). Peter Howson (ASD). Jackson Pollock (Bipolar). Wassily Kandinsky (ASD). Painting outside the lines.

One of the hallmarks of neurodiversity is difficulty in changing focus. That's because the issue being focused on has taken over. Call it a compulsion. Or call it genius. It can be both.

That's why Einstein wasn't always available to have a drink with friends, or even say, "Hi." He had things on his mind. There were questions he wanted to explore, and there was other stuff bubbling up from the back of his head. Bam! $E= mc^2$.

Lewis Carroll was a bit of a loner. Yeah....

Charles Darwin didn't speak much. Okay....

Nikola Tesla wouldn't even come out of his hotel room...

They were busy. They had turned on the creativity. And, they knew it. They knew how to dial it in and write it down. They knew how to submerge themselves in it and create the mindset that was waiting for the spark. *Zot!*

It's *another* Big Bang. Not unlike the first Big Bang, but smaller and more manageable. Certainly creativity is like "Creation." The same little particles that scientists and philosophers posit as being the building blocks of the universe are running our brains. Electrons, and such.

Are they also the building blocks of thoughts? Are there direct connections between the stars and ideas? Are there cute little supernovas deep inside our brains?

Are black holes connecting dimensions into our very skulls? Is that where the big ideas come from?

Maybe. If you're neurodivergent.

An interesting alternative to the Big Bang is the book of Genesis, a blend of mysticism, gossip, faith, and good storytelling. All of that stuff depends on the brain, too. There are facts and archeology—science again—supporting some of them. Mix them with spirits, ghosts, faith healing, miracles, and life everlasting. You'll figure it out.

RELIGION is where "creation" was created. Dreams. Visions. Rapture. Revelation. Prayer. Even reincarnation. Pretty creative thinking. Moses (ASD). Noah (ASD). Samson (ASD). Solomon (ASD). King David (ASD). King Saul (ADHD). Joseph Smith (ADHD). L. Ron Hubbard (ASD). Buddha (ASD). Martin Luther (OCD). The Apostle Paul (Epilepsy).

To be Neurodivergent is to be human. Flaws. Strengths. Inconsistencies. That makes things interesting. It's why so many characters in fiction are given traits of neurodiversity. We enjoy these behaviors in protagonists from Sherlock Holmes to Bart and Lisa Simpson to Dracula and Sheldon. Even Santa Claus.

In particular, we read of wizards who are armed not only with magic, but with exceptional, unusual minds. From Merlin to Gandalf to Hogwarts, fictional sorcerers share characteristics of neurodiversity—the very same traits that can be found in our classrooms. Perhaps the neurodivergent students of today can become the wizards of the future, with skills that can make them heroes in real life.

What used to be fantasy—or magic—is now just everyday life. Abra cadabra... Flight! Electric lights! Talking across distances! With pictures! Medicines! Air conditioning! Who do we have to thank for that? Science fiction writers?

Yes. The best of them. Long before the invention comes the thought. The wish list.

So who puts all those new, interesting thoughts into our books? The same people who think them.

There are sooooo many words. And they can be put in different orders, various sequences of thought fragments that can come together in myriad ways. Make a story. Make a poem. Make a point.

Authors, playwrights, poets, screenwriters, journalists, even bloggers. They freeze thoughts and pass them on, to others.

There are different languages, too, for flavor. Compare notes between cultures. Same? Or not? Or both.

Anybody can write. Some do. Some shouldn't. But some break through. They also break the rules, coming up with new standards, new insights, and new readers.

Someone needs to write technical manuals that are understandable. News writing has to be fair and clear. Advertising and propaganda? Make up your own mind. Influencers? Ptui! There are joke writers whose genius is more effective than most preachers. There's drama and comedy, of course, but to make them work, writers need insight.

WRITERS live inside the brains that create new universes. Authors. Poets. Dramatists. Philosophers. Cartoonists. Even screenwriters. Jules Verne (ADHD). Emily Dickinson (ASD). F. Scott Fitzgerald (ADHD). George Bernard Shaw (ADHD). H.G. Wells (ASD). Agatha Christie (Dyslexia). Edgar Allan Poe (ASD). Leo Tolstoy (ASD). Charles Schultz (ASD). Aldous Huxley (ASD). Jane Austen (ASD). Mark Twain (ASD). James Joyce (ASD). Lewis Carroll (ASD). Dante Alighieri (Epilepsy). Franz Kafka (ASD). Hans Christian Andersen (ASD). Neil Gaiman (ASD*). Steven Cannell (Dyslexia*). George Orwell (ASD). Temple Grandin (ASD*). Alexander Pushkin (ADHD). Virginia Woolf (Bipolar). Percy Bysshe Shelley (ASD). Ernest Hemingway (ADHD). Fannie Flagg (Dyslexia*). Charles Dickens (OCD). Billy Bob Thornton (Dyslexia*). Niccolo Machiavelli (ASD), William Blake (ASD). Francis Ford Coppola (Bipolar*). Mary Shelley (ASD). Rachel Carson (ASD). Fyodor Dostoevsky (ASD). Hugh Wilson (Dyslexia*). Emily Bronte (ASD). Charles Bukowski (Dyslexia). Simone de Beauvoir (ASD), Walt Whitman (ASD). Marcel Proust (OCD). H.P. Lovecraft (ASD). J.R.R. Tolkien (ADHD). Samuel Johnson (Tourette). Peter Mark Roget (OCD). Hermann Hesse (Bipolar). Douglas Adams (ADHD). Garrison Keillor (ASD). Issac Asimov (ASD). Algernon Charles Swinburne (ASD). William Butler Yeats (ASD).

Surprised? Probably not.

* Denotes self-identified.

MUSICIANS touch us in a place we cannot see. Across time and space, from vibrations in the air that fly through electronics and wires until they vibrate different air into our modern ears and hearts. *Da da da DAH!* It's a form of mathematics that can make us soar. Or weep. Or unite our feelings. It's a message from Mozart, or Bach, or Handel, or Kurt Kobain. They take us on a journey. We offer applause in return. Sounds fair.

But it's the thoughts that connect their minds to ours. It's truly crazy. And infinite. See a pattern? Neurodiversity anyone?

Adam Levine (OCD*). Wolfgang Amadeus Mozart (ADHD). Justin Timberlake (OCD*). Billy Eilish (Tourette*). Courtney Love (ASD*). John Lennon (Dyslexia). Cher (Dyslexia*). Will.I.Am (ADHD*). Stevie Wonder (ADHD). Bob Dylan (ASD). James Taylor (ASD*). Florence Welch (DCD*). John Denver (ASD). Justin Beiber (ADHD*). Mel B (ADHD*). Brittany Spears (ASD). Harry Belafonte (Dyslexia). Kurt Kobain (ADHD*). Elvis Presley (ADHD). Ludwig von Beethoven (ADHD). Frank Sinatra (OCD). George Frideric Handel (ADHD). Snoop Dogg (ADHD*). Cole Porter (OCD). Gustav Mahler (ASD). Taylor Swift (ASD). Warren Zevon (OCD*). Richard Strauss (ASD). Ed Sheeran (ASD). Carrie Underwood (ADHD*). Ice Cube (ASD*). Richard Wagner (ADHD). Neil Young (Epilepsy). Joey Ramone (OCD). Johannes Brahms (ASD). Steven Tyler (ADHD). George Gershwin (ADHD). Johann Sebastian Bach (ASD). Franz Schubert (ASD). David Byrne (ASD*). Eminem (ASD*). Dave Grohl (ADHD). Kanye West (ASD*). Katy Perry (OCD). Solange Knowles (ADHD*). Elton John (Epilepsy). Carly Simon (Dyslexia). Axl Rose (Bipolar). Frederic Chopin (Epilepsy).

* Denotes self-identifying.

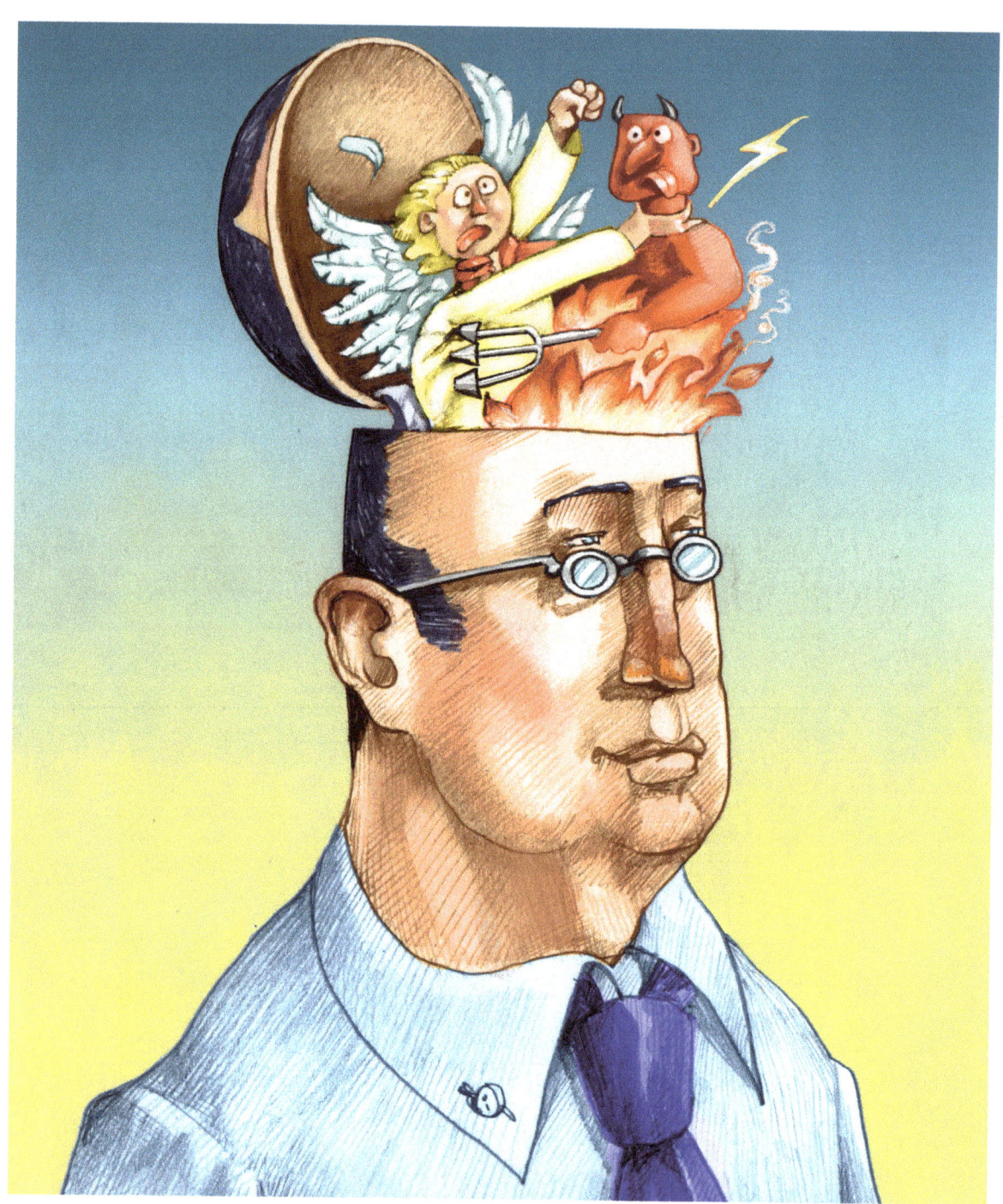

FILMMAKERS make their dreams come true and photograph them. They turn visions into reality into colored shadows that speak. Steven Spielberg (dyslexia*). Alfred Hitchcock (ASD). Tim Burton (ASD*). Stanley Kubrick (ASD). Woody Allen (ASD*). Orson Welles (ASD). Martin Scorsese (Dyslexia*). Spike Lee (Dyslexia*). Quentin Tarantino (Dyslexia*). David Lean (ASD). George Lucas (Dyslexia). Guy Ritchie (Dyslexia). Ridley Scott (ASD). Michael Bay (ASD). David Lynch (ASD). Francis Ford Coppola (Dyslexia). Jerry Lewis (OCD). Guillermo Del Toro (ADHD).

ACTORS lead fictional lives in imaginary worlds and times.

Daniel Radcliffe (DCD*). George C. Scott (ADHD). Henry Winkler (Dyslexia*). Channing Tatum (ADHD*). Emma Watson (OCD*). Ryan Gosling (ADHD*). Zooey Deschanel (ADHD*). Charlie Chaplin (ASD). Mark Ruffalo (ADHD*). Johnny Depp (ADHD*). Woody Harrelson (ADHD). Will Smith (ADHD*). Dan Aykroyd (ASD*). Daryl Hannah (ASD). Anthony Hopkins (ASD*). Dustin Hoffman (ADHD). Jack Nicholson (ADHD). Keira Knightly (Dyslexia). Orlando Bloom (Dyslexia*). Jennifer Love Hewitt (OCD*). Jim Carey (ADHD*). Whoopi Goldberg (ADHD). Eva Longoria (ADHD). Robert Downey Jr. (Bipolar). Danny Glover (Dyslexia*). Cameron Diaz (ADHD*). Seth Rogan (Tourette). Charlize Theron (OCD*). Steve Mc-Queen (Dyslexia). Tom Cruise (Dyslexia*). Leonardo DiCaprio (OCD*). Jessica Alba (OCD*). Buster Keaton (ASD). Megan Fox (ADHD). Alec Baldwin (OCD*). Julianne Moore (OCD). Charlie Sheen (OCD). Jennifer Anniston (Dyslexia). Marlon Brando (ADHD). Vince Vaughn (Dyslexia*). Emily Lloyd (OCD*). Patrick Dempsey (Dyslexia*). Catherine Zeta Jones (bipolar*). Sylvester Stallone (Dyslexia). Keanu Reeves (Dyslexia*). Vince Vaughn (ADHD*). Harrison Ford (OCD*).

* Denotes self-identifying.

There are serious people who propose that creativity comes from other dimensions, which in itself is quite creative. But who knows? There are psychics who claim to see the future or visit with the dearly departed. Some would-be scholars see the long lost civilizations of antiquity with their unknown technologies and connect them to alien communications with earthlings.

On some level those explanations are as satisfying as the notion of chemicals and electricity running our brains with billions of neurons zapping through trillions of cranial connections in a microcosmic simulation of the universe itself.

Certainly their have been mystics and shamans for centuries inducing native trances. Carlos Castenada promoted lucid dreaming in addition to primitive drug rituals. Dreams and visions are prominent in the Bible, leading to revelations and prophecies for Joseph, Daniel, Jacob, the Wise Men, and the apostles Paul and Peter, among others.

There is even a school of thought that neurodiversity is not a genetic misstep, but a step in evolution to a higher level of humanity.

What about the NON-neurodivergents? Where do their ideas come from? They have imaginations, too. They have intellects. They are stimulated in many of the same ways, but everyday logic may be an obstacle. Some problems are just particularly hard, and it takes a divergent mind to keep going deep into uncharted territory. Concepts like cubism and evolution and black holes just don't pop up easily.

Ideas and solutions don't necessarily come when they're needed, and, there's not always time to find a neurodivergent to save the day.

Some turn to alcohol and drugs for inspiration. Hunter S. Thompson and Truman Capote for instance. Maybe you've heard of the Beatles? The list of musicians and drug use is infinite, whether it's to induce creativity or just create havoc. Results are certainly mixed.

There are a lot of Neurotypicals simulating Neurodivergence, searching for ideas.

COMEDIANS look at things kind of funny, on a professional level.

Jim Jeffries (ASD*). Jay Leno (Dyslexia*). Chris Rock (NVLD*). Ellen DeGeneres (OCD). Howie Mandel (OCD*). Robin Williams (ADHD). Tommy Smothers (Dyslexia*). Roseanne Barr (OCD*). Jerry Seinfeld (ASD*). Joan Rivers (ADHD). Johnny Carson (ADHD). Trevor Noah (ADHD). Hannah Gadsby (ASD*). Rachel Feinstein (ADHD). Hasan Minhaj (ADHD). Woody Allen (ASD). Mark Normand (OCD). Brian Regan (OCD). Maria Bamford (OCD). Andy Kaufman (ASD). Michael Palin (ASD). George Carlin (ASD).

A dyslexic, an epileptic, and a autist walk into a bar....

* Denotes self-identifying.

VISIONARIES, REVOLUTIONARIES, & OTHER ASSORTED GENIUSES are true to the neurodivergent type. They are the true free thinkers.

Harriet Tubman (Epilepsy). Erin Brockovich (Dyslexia). David Blaine (ADHD). Christopher Columbus (ADHD). Che Guevara (ADHD). Temple Grandin (ASD*). Howard Stern (OCD*). Dr. Vernon Smith (ASD*). James Carvill (ADHD). Tommy Hilfiger (Dyslexia*). Bobby Fischer (ASD). Greta Thunberg (ASD). Captain James Cook (ASD). Tyra Banks (OCD*). Eleanor Roosevelt (ADHD). Jim Henson (ASD). Paul Allen (ASD). Le Corbusier (ASD). Satoshi Tajiri (ASD). Dr. Vernon Smith (ASD).

Savants

Savants are the pinnacle of neurodiversity. A savant is extremely gifted in one or more ways, but there is usually a corresponding deficit in other ways.

Mostly male, savants are often quite strong in mathematics or music, although there are other types of expertise as well. Many have prodigious memories for minor details. It's interesting that several are blind, and some only developed their abilities after severe head injuries.

Artist Stephen Wiltshire draws large, incredibly detailed and complicated landscapes from memory. Daniel Tammet speaks eleven languages and can recite *pi* to the 22,000th digit. (Who's checking this?) Megasavant Kim Peek has memorized twelve thousand books. Ellen Boudreaux can tell time to the exact second. Jason Padgett sees numbers as fractals and can accurately draw them by hand. Tony Deblois played the piano as a two-year-old and has memorized over 8,000 pieces of music that he can play on twenty different instruments. Gilles Trehim started drawing an imaginary French city at age twelve and has 250 detailed images, plus a book describing the city of Urville. Dr. Thomas "Blind Tom" Wiggins, a former slave, toured with piano concerts playing over 7,000 pieces of music from memory. Temple Grandin thinks in pictures—allowing her to design exceptional equipment for handling livestock—yet she has written multiple books and is a frequent speaker on the subject of autism.

In addition, there are other sculptors, poets, painters, and musicians who showcase incredible talents.

All savants have autism. There are no super-jugglers with Developmental Coordination Disorder or Tourette sufferers cursing exquisitely.

Savants are quite rare, and there are estimated to be fewer than one hundred worldwide.

If you're wondering what it's like to be neurodivergent—or even wondering if *you* are neurodivergent, here's a simple little test for creativity.

It's a blank page. It's blank on both sides, so that if you tear it out, you won't miss any of the rest of this book.

Just write (or draw) anything you want on that page. Anything.

If you're a neurotypical, you might jot down a note or two, or doodle something meaningless, and then you'll turn the page and keep reading. Or, maybe you don't care a whit and you've already turned the page, thus missing the rest of this magnificent text.

But, if you're a neurodivergent, get comfortable. You're going to be here for a while.

True, you can write or draw *anything*, but that's not your nature. You're not going to ruin a perfectly blank piece of paper unless you have something that's worth it.

Or, you may have already torn the page out and thrown it away. A few of you may have even torn it into tiny fragments, like tossing a flurry of blank confetti.

Some of you will have carefully cut the page out with scissors or such, so as not to ruin either the page or the book. Bless your heart.

Still stumped? Indeed, a blank page is a formidable obstacle. Are you up to the challenge? Is it worth the time? But why can't you move on? Damn....

Now if you've been stuck on this page for an hour or more, you should feel free to skip it, earning yourself the honorary title of Quasi-Neurodivergent.

For the rest of you, each time you read this page, we suggest that you check one of the boxes below. Once you've checked all the boxes, you should feel free to turn the page and get on with your life.

☐ ☐ ☐ ☐ ☐ ☐ ☐ ☐ ☐ ☐ ☐ ☐ ☐ ☐

☐ ☐ ☐ ☐ ☐ ☐ ☐ ☐ ☐ ☐ ☐ ☐ ☐ ☐

Now that the test is over, how do you feel that you did? Are you proud of your work, or do you have lingering thoughts about your result?

Do you want to show it off? Or, do you want to rework it in some way? Even if you've discarded it, it's still nagging at you, isn't it? At least a little bit.

What would Leonardo da Vinci have done with that page? You should be ashamed.

What would Mozart have done with the time you wasted thinking about it? A symphony? Or just a jingle?

James Joyce would have both wasted the page and transformed it into something magnificent and obtuse. Why couldn't you do that?

From time to time, you will think back on that blank page for the rest of your life, wondering—why couldn't I have done more?

Here are two possible reasons.

1. You are not neurodivergent. (You just don't care.)

2. You are neurodivergent. (Maybe you care too much.)

Still thinking about it? That's the thing about creativity. You can't find it when you're looking for it. It's there, lurking somewhere in the recesses of your cranium, but it's a bit like your cat. It doesn't always respond to its name. True, we rely on creativity, but we can't count on it.

Can you count to ten without thinking of an elephant? Probably not. At least not now. That means you aren't completely in control of your own mind. And that's the way creativity works. It's a part of your mind that you can't control, no matter how much you need it.

Sometimes it works. It's usually too little, too late, but we're grateful for whatever breakthrough happens. But—looking back on almost every creative solution to a problem is the same question. Why didn't I see that before?

It's like we always have to wait for tomorrow to solve yesterday's problems, when we really need the solution *today*.

What makes one lyric simply meaningless, while an equally meaningless lyric becomes timeless? Genius. That's it. Cole Porter's thoughts were different from whatever you wrote on the blank page. (We'll check back in a century to see which one has held up.)

So there's something going on in those "different" brains that is, well, *different*. We can't see it in an MRI, or even an autopsy, but we can see it in the way it makes other people smile at a melody or nod at an essay or laugh at a joke.

Is creativity simply mystical? Is it just something we believe in, like alchemy or astrology or religion or multivitamins?

No. We know it's the brain. We can point to the Parietal Lobe and the Medulla Oblongata and the Occipital Lobe, but we can't point to inspiration. And we can't separate the dyslexia from the symphony. We can't pinpoint where on the spectrum that brilliant computer code comes from.

We can't isolate the neurons that make someone's attention flit incessantly from one thing to another, then hyperfocus on something else.

And that brings us back to the neurodivergent folks. They've got inspiration on steroids. They can turn it on. Properly aimed, it's a tool. Sometimes they can't even stop it.

We owe them respect, not derision. For centuries there have been insults aimed at them. Dimwit. Idiot. Lunatic. Weirdo. Ad infinitum.

Maybe now there's a new dig. Neurotypical.

Creativity is not just dreaming big thoughts by geniuses. Neurodiversity is inclusive. They are all around us, with unexpected good ideas, big and small.

If Neurodiversity causes Creativity, what do we do with this knowledge?

Listen to the neurodivergent! Offer acceptance. And more. Acknowledgment. Support. Resources. Tools. Information. Encouragement. Celebrate them. Get out of their way! Spread the word!

And don't wait until they're dead to call them a genius....

The nuts, nerds, and savants listed previously are only a selection of neurodivergent superstars from posterity and the present, but we should be looking forward. There are always more new folks in the pipeline. Neurodiversity is no different.

Looking back through history, we shouldn't just reap the productivity from the neurodivergent geniuses—their inventions, the symphonies, the insights. We should learn from their other experiences. Understand the roadblocks they faced. Get past the tics and the failings—just like they did—and grin at the successes. Share them widely. Make it easier for the next....

There are books that list symptoms and all the things that go wrong in neurodivergent brains. Medical books. Psychology books. Self-help books. There should be more books that open doors—and minds. Is neurodiversity a disability, or a path?

Today a new generation faces the same problems, the same environment, the same teasing, blockages, obstacles, ridicule, stupidity, attitudes. Heartbreaks. There will be multitudes of them—all struggling—but those are individual struggles in individual minds.

We have the ability—the obligation—to change the world they're emerging into—to share an enlightened collective mind.

We can affect the environment of schools, from teachers to other students to parents, and make the classrooms hospitable. We can offer recognition instead of drawing the shutters. We can embrace difficulties together.

The potential creativity of this new "hive mind" is unlimited. We don't turn our backs on gold mines or oil wells.

For all the promise of artificial intelligence, "real" intelligence will draw from deep within us and ride our dreams.

This is the heart of creativity.

THE END

Good news! If you were one of the readers who opted to tear out the blank page with the creativity test, you're going to need another piece of blank paper.

We have provided an endless supply of such pages on our website at: *www.cosworthpublishing.com/catalog.html*. There you can buy an unlimited number of identical books, each complete with a matching blank page as a replacement.

This provides a wonderful opportunity to express your creativity. Show us your best stuff.

About the Author

Jimmy Huston (ASD, OCD, ADHD, DCD, NVLD, Dyslexia, Dyscalculia, Tourette, Bipolar) grew up in Athens, Georgia, before neurodivergence had been invented. Now that he lives in California, where it's mandatory, he's finally growing into it. Just ask his wife or dog.

Cover faces. 1. Elon Musk. 2. Charles Darwin. 3. Pablo Picasso. 4. George Washington. 5. Socrates. 6. Salvador Dali. 7. Mark Twain. 8. Immanuel Kant. 9. Stephen Hawking. 10. Nikola Tesla. 11. Simone de Beauvoir 12. Niccolo Machiavelli. 13. Thomas Edison. 14. Bill Gates. 15. Albert Einstein. 16. Marie Curie. 17. Leonardo da Vinci. 18. Emily Dickinson. 19. Ernest Hemingway. 20. Hypatia of Alexandria. 21. Edgar Allan Poe. 22. Walt Whitman. 23. Jules Verne. 24. Isaac Newton. 25. Oscar Wilde. 26. George Gershwin. 27. Galileo Galilei. 28. Dante Alighieri.

More Books from Jimmy Huston

www.cosworthpublishing.com

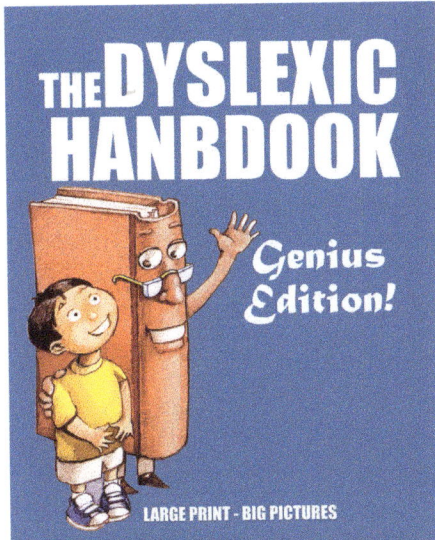

THE **DYSLEXIC HANBDOOK**

Genius Edition!

LARGE PRINT - BIG PICTURES

THE **OCD** FUNBOOK

REALLY?

The Attention Deficit Disorder Hyperactive Cookbook

Puzzle Edition

Autism for Beginners

Surfing the Spectrum

The **I Hate to Read** Book

Jimmy Huston

...and **I Hate Math 2**

Who Needs It?

Jimmy Huston

Baby's First Instruction Manual

PG-½

How To Be the Center of the Universe

How to **Write This Book!**

You're going to be the author.

_____
(Write your name here.)

The Snake Test

☐ True? ☐ False? ☐ Maybe

CUSSING for KIDS!

Etiquette for the Profane

More Books from Jimmy Huston

www.cosworthpublishing.com

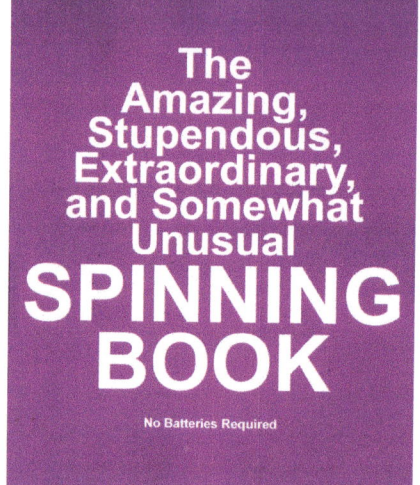

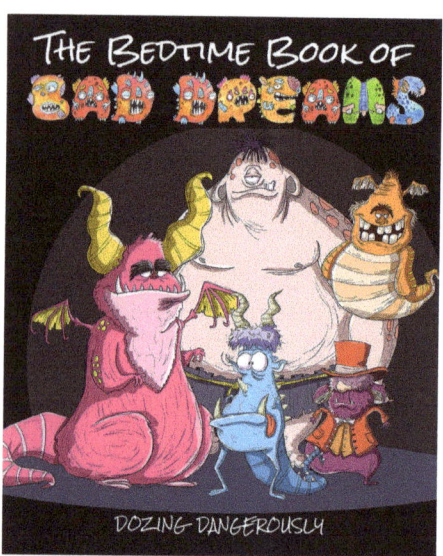

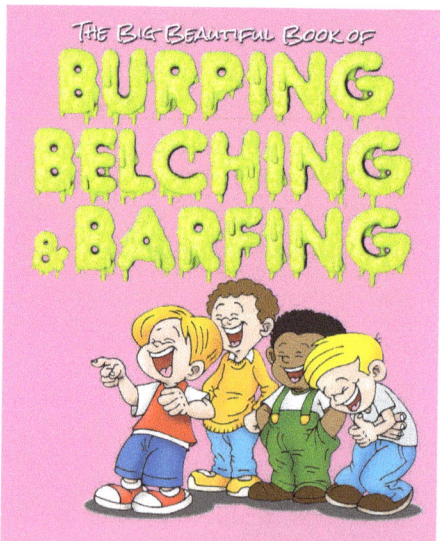

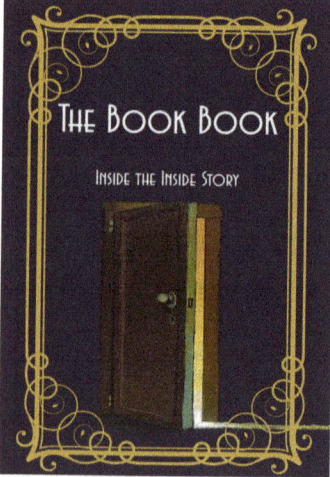

Books for Grownups from Cosworth Publishing

www.cosworthpublishing.com

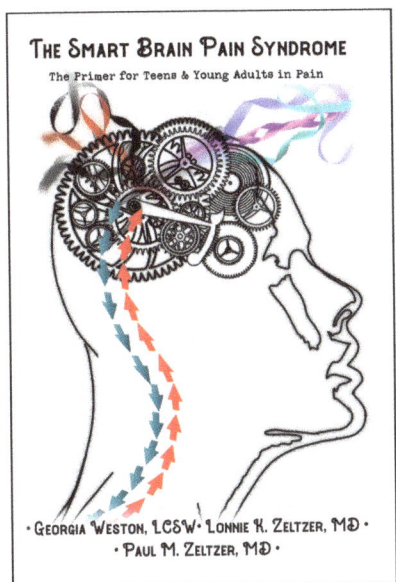

A groundbreaking new book. Three experts explain chronic pain to teens and parents, including using creative outlets to displace the pain.

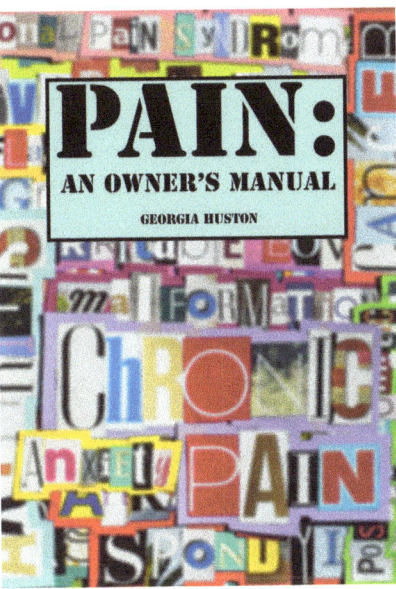

A young pain victim's inspirational and informative conversations with a variety of pain sufferers and specialists. Doctors should read this at their own risk.

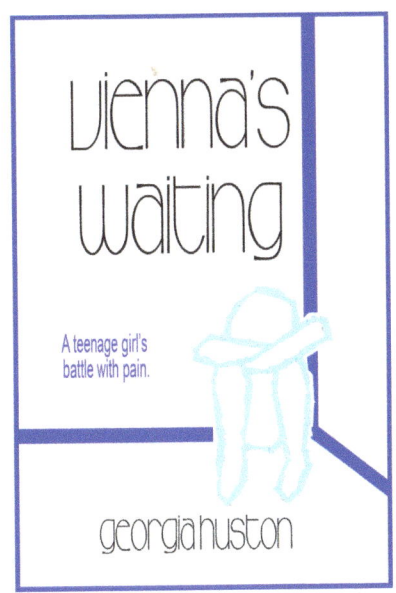

At 14, Georgia developed mysterious chronic pain. This book chronicles that dark time and follows her inspirational journey back to health and happiness.

A practical guide for the person who is confronted by the possible suicide of a friend or family member.

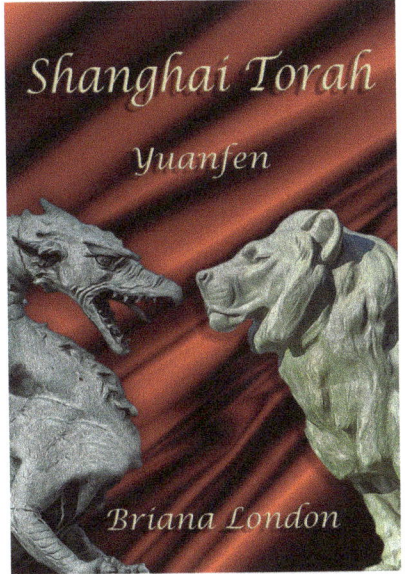

A young Jewish scribe flees WWII Europe with his in-progress Torah, escaping into China under Japanese occupation.

AUDIOBOOK

A powerful reading of Georgia's harrowing experiences as a young teen suffering chronic pain. Hearing it all out loud brings new power and meaning to this true-life story.

Thanks for buying, borrowing, or swiping this wonderful book.

At Cosworth Publishing we truly appreciate that, and in return, we'd like to offer you one of our E-books absolutely free—and worth every penny.

Just let us know that you want it, and we'll make sure that you get it. Let us know which book you read so we don't send you the same one.

Send an email to *office@cosworthpublishing.com*.

Then, from time to time, we will let you know via email when we have a new book that you might be interested in.

We won't do that very often because we're basically pretty lazy, and we don't produce very many new books.

Reviews are usually appreciated.

Libros de Jimmy Huston

www.cosworthpublishing.com

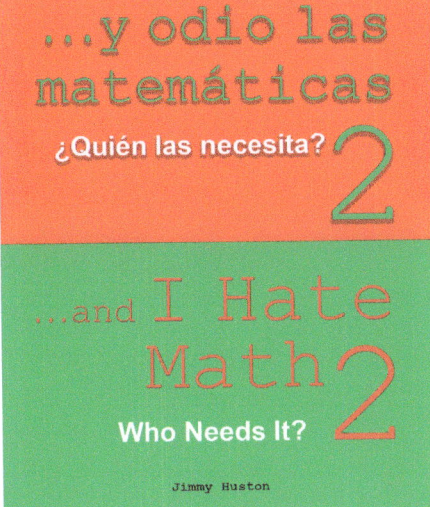